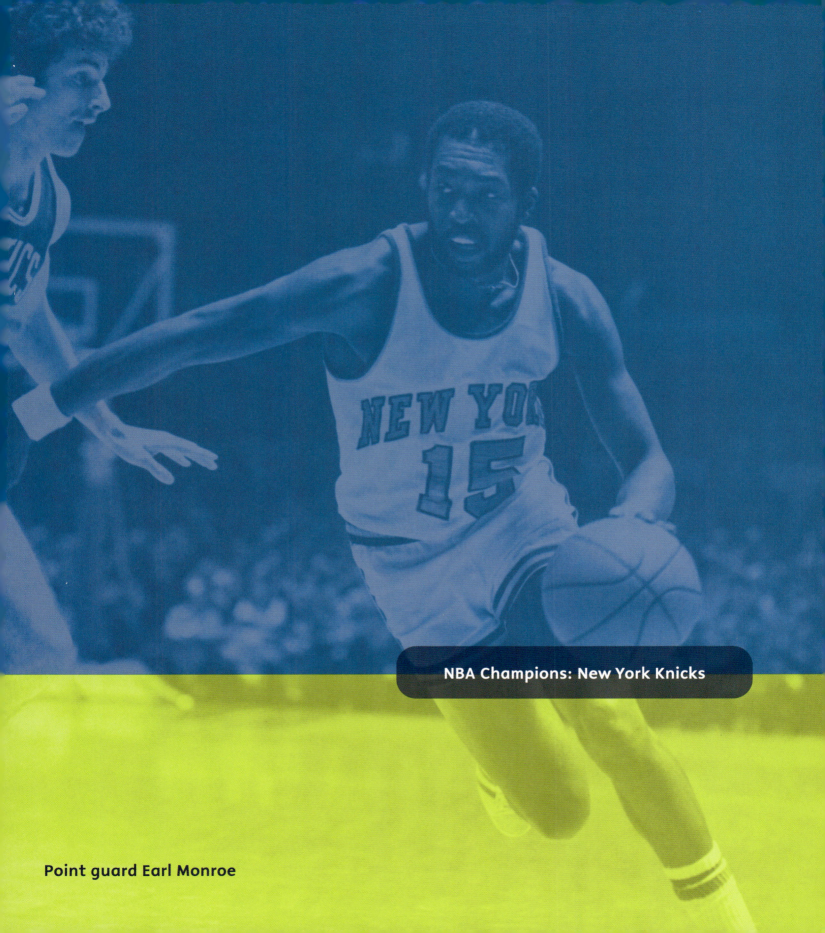

NBA Champions: New York Knicks

Point guard Earl Monroe

Shooting guard Evan Fournier

NBA CHAMPIONS

NEW YORK KNICKS

BY JAMES BARRY

CREATIVE EDUCATION / CREATIVE PAPERBACKS

Published by Creative Education and Creative Paperbacks
P.O. Box 227, Mankato, Minnesota 56002
Creative Education and Creative Paperbacks are imprints of
The Creative Company
www.thecreativecompany.us

Art Direction by Tom Morgan
Book production by Graham Morgan
Edited by Grace Cain

Images by Getty Images/ Al Bello, 10, Alex Goodlett, 2, Focus On Sport, 3, 7, 24, FPG, 4, George Long, 19, Jim Cummins, 1, Mitchell Leff, 20, Nathaniel S. Butler, 16, NBA Photos, 15, Tom Berg, 5, Wen Roberts, cover, 12; JIM YOUNG/Reuters, 6; Newscom/ DAVID MAXWELL, cover; Unsplash/ Triston Dunn, 9
Every effort has been made to contact copyright holders for material reproduced in this book. Any omissions will be rectified in subsequent printings if notice is given to the publisher.

Copyright © 2025 Creative Education, Creative Paperbacks
International copyright reserved in all countries. No part of this book may be reproduced in any form without written permission from the publisher.

Library of Congress Cataloging-in-Publication Data

Names: Barry, James (Author of children's books) author.
Title: New York Knicks / by James Barry.
Description: Mankato, MN : Creative Education and Creative Paperbacks, [2025] | Series: Creative sports. NBA champions | Includes index. | Audience: Ages 7-10 | Audience: Grades 2-3 | Summary: "Elementary-level text and dynamic sports photos highlight the NBA championship wins of the New York Knicks, plus sensational players associated with the professional basketball team such as Jalen Brunson"— Provided by publisher.
Identifiers: LCCN 2024018496 (print) | LCCN 2024018497 (ebook) | ISBN 9798889892618 (library binding) | ISBN 9781682776278 (paperback) | ISBN 9798889893721 (ebook)
Subjects: LCSH: New York Knickerbockers (Basketball team)—Juvenile literature.
Classification: LCC GV885.52.N4 B27 2025 (print) | LCC GV885.52.N4 (ebook) | DDC 796.323/64097471—dc23/eng/20240426
LC record available at https://lccn.loc.gov/2024018496
LC ebook record available at https://lccn.loc.gov/2024018497

Printed in China

Power forward Nathaniel Clifton

Center Patrick Ewing

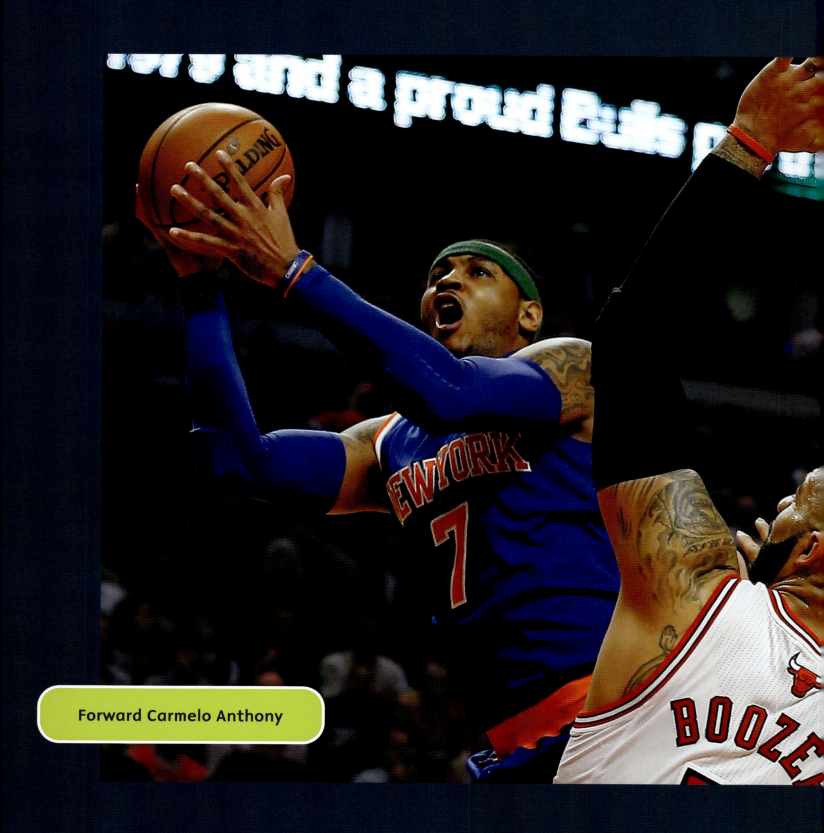

Forward Carmelo Anthony

CONTENTS

Home of the Knicks	8
Naming the Knicks	13
Knicks History	14
Other Knicks Stars	18
About the Knicks	22
Glossary	23
Index	24

Home of the Knicks

New York City is the biggest and busiest city in the United States. The city has a lot of nicknames, including "The Big Apple." It has an **arena** called Madison Square Garden. It is the home of a basketball team called the Knicks.

NBA CHAMPIONS

Guard Jalen Brunson

The New York Knicks are part of the National Basketball Association (NBA). They play in the Atlantic Division. That's part of the Eastern Conference. Two of their biggest **rivals** are the Brooklyn Nets and the Boston Celtics.

Center Willis Reed

Naming the Knicks

Colonists who came to New York sometimes wore short pants. These became known as knickerbockers. The name chosen for the basketball team was the New York Knickerbockers. A cartoon of a man wearing that style of pants was used on signs for the team. "Knicks" is short for Knickerbockers.

Knicks History

The Knicks started playing in 1946. Forward Harry Gallatin was a great scorer and **rebounder**. He helped the Knicks reach the NBA Finals in 1951, 1952, and 1953. They did not win a championship.

In 1967, William "Red" Holzman became coach. His teams practiced hard. They played tough defense. Strong center Willis Reed led the Knicks to their first championship in 1970. Then he led them to their second **title** in 1973.

Forward Harry Gallatin

Center Patrick Ewing

After many losing seasons, New York chose center Patrick Ewing with the first pick in the 1985 NBA Draft. For 15 years, he pushed the Knicks to the top of the NBA. Fans attended Madison Square Garden to cheer on the home team. Ewing's Knicks lost in the Finals in 1994 and 1999.

Other Knicks Stars

Knicks fans have cheered for many great players. High-scoring guard Richie Guerin made six straight All-Star teams with the Knicks. Flashy guard Walt Frazier was a great scorer, passer, and **defender**. He was a big part of the championship teams of the 1970s.

Fast-moving small forward Bernard King led the NBA in scoring during the 1984–85 season. In the

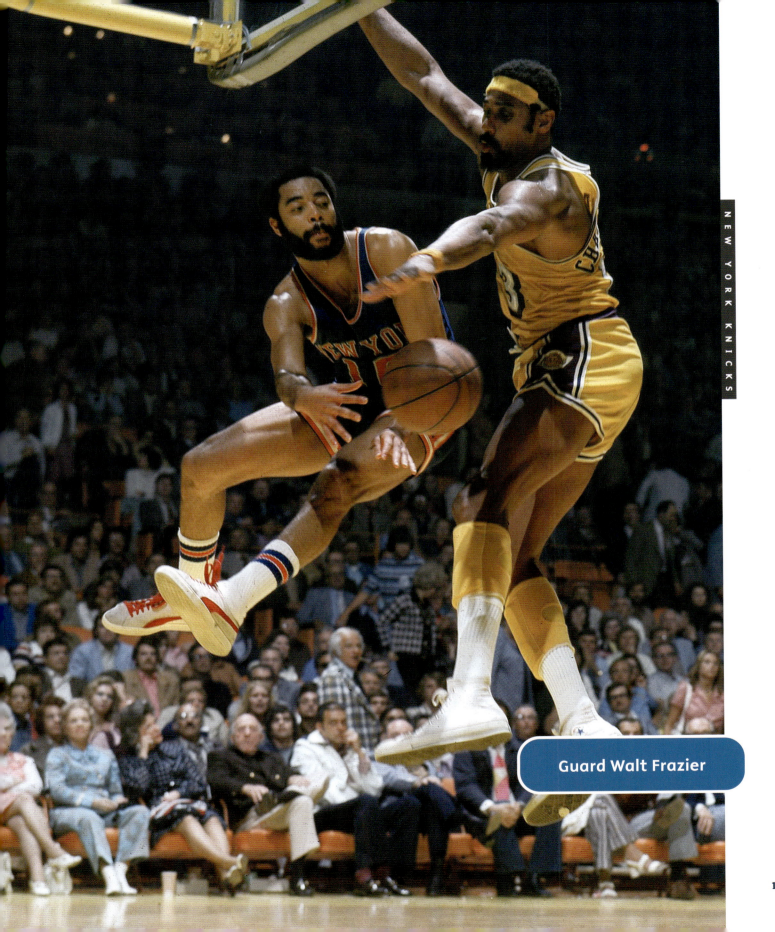

Guard Walt Frazier

NEW YORK KNICKS

19

Small forward OG Anunoby

NBA CHAMPIONS

1990s, John Starks sank long three-point shots and slammed highflying dunks. Hot-shooting forward Carmelo Anthony was the team's top scorer in the 2010s.

Skillful guard Jalen Brunson joined the Knicks in 2022. He became an all-star in his second season in New York. In 2023, athletic small forward OG Anunoby was traded to the Knicks. He's one of the NBA's best defenders. Fans hope he will help bring another championship to New York soon!

About the Knicks

First season: 1946–47

Conference/division: Eastern Conference, Atlantic Division

Team colors: blue, orange, silver, black, and white

Home arena: Madison Square Garden

NBA CHAMPIONSHIPS:

1970, 4 games to 3 over Los Angeles Lakers

1973, 4 games to 1 over Los Angeles Lakers

TEAM WEBSITE:

https://www.nba.com/knicks/

Glossary

arena—a large building with seats for spectators, where sports games and entertainment events are held

defender—a player who stops the other team from scoring

rebounder—a player who catches and controls the ball after a missed shot

rival—a team that plays extra hard against another team

title—another word for championship

NBA CHAMPIONS

Center Willis Reed

Index

Anthony, Carmelo, 6, 21
Anunoby, OG, 20, 21
Brunson, Jalen, 10, 21
Clifton, Nathaniel, 4
Ewing, Patrick, 5, 16, 17
Fournier, Evan, 2
Frazier, Walt, 18, 19
Gallatin, Harry, 14, 15
Guerin, Richie, 18
Holzman, William "Red", 14
King, Bernard, 18
Madison Square Garden, 8, 17, 22
Monroe, Earl, 1
Reed, Willis, 12, 14, 24
Starks, John, 21
team name, 13